JONAH

Following God's Call When You'd Rather Run Away

CHARLIE GRIMES

Library of Congress Control Number: 2025916923

ISBN: 979-8-9992022-0-8

Charlie Grimes
1206 Cecilia Dr NW, Strasburg, OH 44680

800.927.4196 · carlisleprinting.com
2673 Township Road 421 · Sugarcreek, Ohio 44681

ENDORSEMENTS

Praise for "Jonah: Following God's Call When You'd Rather Run Away":

"Charlie Grimes is a gifted communicator, coach, and pastor. We are fortunate to have this book on Jonah that resulted from the studies he did for a powerful sermon series. I especially commend it to you for its life application at every step for both believers and non-believers, even if you haven't ever spent time in the belly of a whale. The reflection questions and prayers also lead to a deeper engagement with Jonah's themes of rebellion, grace, and forgiveness."

Pastor Matt Hamsher, MDiv, Executive Director, Evana Network

"In a time in history when it seems everyone is in pursuit of happiness, my friend Charlie wrote with courage about what it means to pursue faithfulness to Almighty God. As Charlie writes, "Sometimes what concerns me is different than what concerns God." Being a servant of God is not the same as expecting God to serve me. God is using Charlie to lead us from the path of "what concerns me" to the path of "what concerns God."

Pastor Jim Bartholomew, Dayspring Christian Fellowship, Massillon, OH.

"Charlie Grimes' Jonah: Following God's Call When You'd Rather Run Away is a heartfelt, honest, and deeply relatable journey through the book of Jonah. With clarity and conviction, Charlie helps us wrestle with God's mercy, our comfort, and the unsettling truth that grace isn't just for us—it's for those we struggle to love. This is a powerful resource for anyone longing to align their heart with God's (and may be grieving the times when we have fiercely resisted)."

Mr. Nate Holten, MDiv, Superintendent, Central Christian School, Kidron, OH

"Pastor Grimes challenges the reader to embrace a deeper understanding of a life of obedience, forgiveness, and divine grace through the examination of the truths found in the Book of Jonah. Each chapter provides opportunity for application, reflection, and prayer, ideal for the novice and mature Christ-follower, individual reader, or group study."

Ms. Tanya Hockman, MA, Director of Athletics, Malone University, Canton, OH

"This book offers a fresh and compelling exploration of the timeless story of Jonah, bringing new depth and insight to one of the most complex and relatable figures in the Bible. With clarity, wisdom, and deep respect for Scripture, Charlie unpacks Jonah's journey—from a lens he is all too familiar with "running," running From, Back To, With, and Against God. Whether you're familiar with the story or encountering it anew, this book invites readers into a deeper understanding of the depths of God's ever-pursuing love. It is a thoughtful and engaging read for anyone seeking to grow in their relationship with God."

Dr. Chris Abrams, Dean of Student Affairs, Heidelberg University, Tiffin, OH

"Charlie takes the familiar story of Jonah and brings it to new life with a touch of relatability. He breaks the story into short, bite-sized sections with space to pause, reflect, and pray. With helpful background details and a teacher's voice, Charlie dives into big ideas like God's grace, forgiveness, and second chances, without skipping the hard truths we need to hear. Whether you're running from something or figuring out your faith, this book reminds you that God never gives up on you. It is honest, hopeful, and a great guide for anyone wanting to grow closer to God."

Mr. Sean Miller, Science Educator, Lake Center Christian School, Hartville, OH

"An excellent read which puts the book of Jonah in a perspective that is easy to understand and relate to. It offers hermeneutical insights that are refreshingly applicable and biblically rooted."

Pastor Nathan Stjernholm, Team Pastor, Smithville Mennonite Church, Smithville, OH

"If you've ever said, 'God, I'm not ready,' or 'God, I messed up,' Jonah understands. If you've ever felt far from where God wants you to be, this book is for you. Charlie uses Jonah's story to skillfully show that God doesn't cancel us when we make mistakes. He redirects us. And you can encounter God's love... regardless of how far you've drifted. So whether you are running, repenting, or returning, Jonah's journey is just the inspiration you need."

Pastor Dan Owolabi, Executive Director, Branches Worldwide, Author of Authentic Leadership, Wooster, OH

"Generation upon generation of God's people have spent time sharing the account of Jonah from the perspective of onlookers– safe to enjoy, reflect, and critique. In this book, Charlie takes us by the hand as a pastor and coach to lead us into the storyline where we must face our own Nineveh, our God of unwavering love, and the brokenness of our own hearts. Within the story, space is made for our own confession and conversion so we can move forward with God into the big story He is still writing in this world."

Pastor Craig Strasbaugh, MDiv, Team Pastor, Kidron Mennonite Church, Kidron, OH

"Running with God in a world filled with busyness, selfishness, and distractions can be difficult. This book offers both encouragement and challenges by drawing parallels between Jonah's journey and our own experiences. Whether you're a student in a youth group or in your adult career, Jonah's life provides valuable lessons that can be applied to your own life."

Tyler and Kathryn Moomaw, Public School Educators, Breakthrough Schools, Cleveland, OH

"Pastor Charlie brings a lifetime of experiences to the popular story of Jonah from the Old Testament. With clear storytelling and an easy-to-read style, the story comes alive with wisdom that Christian young people can apply to deepen their walk with the Lord. Jonah's story might remind you of your own challenges, and this book helps each of us gain insights into life that spur us to grow in faith and positively impact those around us!"

Mr. Mark Seymour, MBA, President of Christian School Association of Greater Harrisburg (CSAGH), Hershey, PA

ACKNOWLEDGMENTS

This first book in the *Dare to Believe* series, is dedicated to the congregation at Walnut Creek Mennonite Church in beautiful Holmes County, Ohio. This historical church's hardworking and generous people have loved me and supported me to become more of what God desires for me, personally and vocationally. Due to their gracious love and encouragement, I have grown and matured dramatically in pastoral ministry.

I also praise my wife and partner in life, Wendy, for her patience, wisdom, and administrative gifts. She has kept my life on track toward Jesus in so many practical ways. I'm forever grateful to my daughters, Shannon, Katie, and Leah, as well as their husbands, Jon, Tyler, and Caleb, for their constant encouragement and love. In many ways, I have written these books to bless my grandchildren, Ryder and Callum, and three more who are yet to be born while I write this volume! I love you, my dear children, and pray God's blessing and care upon your lives forever!

No book like this is produced without excellent guidance and supportive editing. Many thanks to Elaine Starner for her partnership, advice, and encouragement. Many thanks also to Maria Kline and the great team at Carlisle Printing. They were patient, kindhearted and so supportive through the design and formatting phases. A huge thank-you also to Nicole and Katherine Troyer, friends from Walnut Creek Mennonite, for their editing and review!

You will notice four outstanding sketches within the chapters. Many thanks to Caeden Hershberger, Lydia Miller, and Clairen Varga (all high school artists) for their excellent contributions.

I also give a hearty shout-out to many mentors and friends: Pastors Jim Bartholomew, Jeff Bargerstock, Jay Conn, Matt Yoder, and Owen Miller; Dr. Shane Johnson, Dr. Chris Abrams, Rev. Randy Heckert, Dr. Greg Linville; my classmates and faculty of Ashland Theological Seminary; Brian Miller, Conrad Mast, and many more. Thanks for your constant encouragement to dream big, live simply, and love deeply.

PREFACE

Here is your only warning: I am not a theologian. I have been in church life for about 40 years and studied the Bible quite a lot. However, I humbly acknowledge that countless men and women are more intelligent and have much more wisdom than I will ever have. I'm a friend of Jesus. I am a follower who has felt His forgiveness, love, hope, and purpose. I want everyone I can reach to know Him more. That often happens when we study and digest the powerful truths found in the Bible.

I am an encourager, too. I want the book you hold to be more than just a collection of words. I want it to be a guide, a coach that comes alongside you, giving courage and inspiring you through God's Holy Spirit to step into whatever He has asked you to do with your life. That takes guts. Obeying God's instructions for your life will be a risk. You'll be tempted to run away. So many other "authorities" would want you to do many different things. Self-serving things. I want to "dare" you to do this, Dare to Believe.

This book might challenge you. Sometimes, you may feel comfortable with your life and its direction, but as you continue reading, you may encounter parts of the story that provoke more profound reflection. You might even find yourself questioning your maturity. This discomfort is part of the process of becoming more self-aware. Just as God deeply offended Jonah, this story might challenge your perceptions. God's act of loving and forgiving a city of evil and selfish people was outrageous to Jonah. He didn't realize that deep down, he was no better than those people. Neither are we. I haven't done my job if you aren't prompted to grow closer to Jesus through the self-reflection this story encourages.

My goal is to challenge your notions of what it means to obey God. Let us wrestle with what God has designed us to do: trust Him more. If we are willing, God will stretch us, and we will discover a new depth of faith in our lives!

INTRODUCTION

If you are like me, your first introduction to the story of the prophet Jonah was read from a little children's Bible. A big fish (or whale) swallowed him. As a child, I was frightened by the storm, frightened by the whale, and even scared by the reputation of the Ninevites, who were known for their cruelty and wickedness.

Many people today doubt that this story is true. They contend that various details within this book don't add up correctly. I can understand that. Even if you have concluded that the narrative in Jonah is just too outrageous to be fact, I hope you can agree that even as a fantasy story Jonah or someone else came up with, it can have value in teaching, admonishing, and guiding us in our faithfulness. I believe this story is more than a family-friendly fairy tale. I believe this story is possible and has tremendous value for our faith. Even though it is only four chapters long, it is one of the Bible's most unique and fascinating texts. In reading this book, I hope you will discover how interesting and helpful it is for our lives today. Get your spiritual wetsuit on because we are heading into the belly of a fish!

Traditionally, the book is considered to have been written by the prophet Jonah himself, mentioned in 2 Kings 14:25. The book's personal nature, especially the prayer in chapter two, suggests that Jonah wrote this as a "memoir." He had firsthand knowledge of all the events, so he captured this as his "testimony."

God called Jonah to do something exceedingly difficult. Repentance and forgiveness are significant themes within the story, seen in Jonah's relationship with God, the repentance shown by those living in Nineveh, and God's response to their repentance. The story will eventually show God's concern and love for all people.

Jonah was born in Gath-Hepher, a region of the northern kingdom of Israel, right near Galilee. We know another great prophet who also came from Galilee. (It was Jesus, by the way!) Jonah is often called the "reluctant prophet." His name meant "dove." Interestingly, a dove is also a symbol of peace and the presence of the Holy Spirit.

This book begins with divine communication. Turn that page and let us start our wonderful journey through this incredible story.

TABLE OF CONTENTS

RUNNING AWAY FROM GOD

The word of the Lord came to Jonah, son of Amittai: (Jonah 1:1)

Jonah is considered a prophet. He was just a regular guy, though, very much like you and me. God gives insight and truth to people so they can speak from God's perspective. God can also provide us with understanding, and we should be careful to obey God when He speaks to us. Jonah spoke on God's behalf many times, so it is not unusual for Jonah that this book begins with a "word from the Lord."

This word from God was pretty unique. It was special because of the specific place God sent Jonah and what God asked him to do while he was there.

"Go to the great city of Nineveh and preach against it, because its wickedness has come up before me." (Jonah 1:2)

The mention of Nineveh may not mean much to us today, but it certainly would have meant something to Jonah. Nineveh was a city of approximately 120,000 people. In that time, in the eighth century B.C., the city was considered massive and was the capital of the Assyrian Empire. The Assyrians were known for their brutality; they murdered and pillaged their way throughout the Middle East. They were considered the bullies of their time. As a result, Nineveh was the symbolic home of everything evil, hateful, and idolatrous. Jonah may have envisioned it with black smokestacks and human sacrifices. This would be the last place a non-Assyrian person would want to go, and the Ninevites were the last people any Jewish person would like to speak to.

And to top it all off, Jonah's people (the Hebrew people) were some of the Assyrian victims who had suffered the most. The Assyrians attacked and looted both the kingdoms of Judah and Israel, wiping out ten of the original twelve tribes of Jacob. This was a horrible part of their history, yet Jonah was instructed to bring a message of conviction, peace, and God's presence to the great and dark city. It seems that Jonah could not even fathom obeying that assignment.

We might compare Jonah being sent to Nineveh to a Jewish person being sent to Nazi Germany in about 1940. Jonah was not just being sent to a place of wickedness, but he was being sent there to tell all of them to repent of their evil ways. Can you imagine? God sent Jonah to stand up to the oppressors and victimizers of his people; he was sent to let the Ninevite people know that God was angry with them, but He was giving them a chance to turn their lives around.

The first simple lesson from this story is: God may ask you to do things you do not want to do.

GOD MAY ASK YOU TO DO THINGS YOU DO NOT WANT TO DO.

God's instruction to Jonah may have seemed crazy. Jonah may have seen this as an impossible

2

request. Given all he knew about Nineveh and the Assyrians, he did what normal people would do: He ran away!

Remember what Jonah's name meant? It was "dove." He was supposed to live up to his name, which meant peace and God's presence. Instead, that dove flew the coop!

But Jonah ran away from the Lord and headed for Tarshish. He went down to Joppa, where he found a ship bound for that port. After paying the fare, he went aboard and sailed for Tarshish to flee from the Lord. (Jonah 1:3)

Joppa was a seaport on the east side of the Mediterranean. Jonah bought a ticket on a ship heading for a place called Tarshish, "to flee from the Lord." Most Bible scholars believe this city, Tarshish, was in southern Spain, on the opposite side of the Mediterranean Sea! In some ways, it was the end of the known world. It was the kind of place you go to really get away. It was the exact opposite direction of Nineveh. Nineveh was on land to the north and east of Joppa. Tarshish was as far west as you could travel!

God told Jonah to go east; he went west. God sent him to Nineveh, a dark place of terror, but instead, Jonah booked a getaway at an all-inclusive resort on the other side of the world!

It was as if Jonah said, "Sure God, I do believe in you, but I'm not going to do what you ask me to do."

We may also have said something like this to God at some point in our lives: "I will go to church; I will pray and worship; I will give some money; I will try not to do the bad stuff, but I have my limits. I am not becoming a pastor, missionary, or anything crazy!"

Another lesson we can learn from this story is: We often run to odd and unsafe places.

WE OFTEN RUN TO ODD AND UNSAFE PLACES.

We often have the deepest regrets when we realize we were running away from something God wanted us to do. I hesitated to become a pastor for about 30 years! God was patient with me, but that's a story for another time. Jonah went through some complicated things, and I think he may have looked back and asked, "What was I thinking?" I believe Jonah wrote this story to teach us about obeying God. Maybe you can relate.

A lesson to remember: You can always find a boat sailing in the wrong direction if you really want one.

YOU CAN ALWAYS FIND A BOAT SAILING IN THE WRONG DIRECTION IF YOU REALLY WANT ONE.

Very few of us have verbally received God's direct, prophet-style message. We may never receive instructions directing us into the heart of a bloodthirsty empire either. But even so, we too have our Ninevehs. God was entrusting Jonah with an incredibly special, exceedingly dangerous assignment. Though our calling might be far less dramatic, there are places where we are called to go, as well as situations and people that the Holy Spirit nudges us toward, but we cannot bring ourselves to go.

God may have called you to forgive someone who has hurt you deeply. He might be asking you to tell the truth or to show love to someone who has caused you deep pain and grief, someone you cannot imagine forgiving. Some of us see injustice and pain in the world, and God may want us to do something about it. Our Nineveh might need to be confronted, but we are too afraid to do it.

Finally, it might even be something about us—a sin, fault, or failure that we hide from everyone. Like Jonah, we would much rather put all our energy and resources into escape. We may use avoidance, such as running away as Jonah did. We try to avoid the situation forever. Our avoidance is not as apparent as Jonah's. Today, as a society, are we eating, drinking, gaming, binge-watching, and scrolling our way away from God's call on our lives? There are so many distractions. For every call to Nineveh in our lives, a ticket to Tarshish is also available.

I am guessing you can relate. We all have our zones of extreme discomfort. We all probably have our Nineveh. We cannot bring ourselves to go there. We will not do it because we see it as impossible, so we run away! We have our Tarshish, too, our preferred methods of escape. We take the ticket to Tarshish, board the boat, and try to get as far away from God as possible. Like Jonah, we will find out that: You can try to run from God, but you cannot outrun God.

Then the Lord sent a great wind on the sea, and such a violent storm arose that the ship threatened to break up. (Jonah 1:4)

No sooner had the crew set sail than God sent a strong storm that could break the ship into sticks and splinters. Jonah thought he could run, but God was already ahead of him, threatening to tear that ship apart to get Jonah back on track. The crew was terrorized and tried everything to escape the storm.

Here is another important lesson we need to understand: When we run away from God, life begins to unravel.

WHEN WE RUN AWAY FROM GOD, LIFE BEGINS TO UNRAVEL.

All the sailors were afraid, and each cried out to his god. And they threw the cargo into the sea to lighten the ship. But Jonah had gone below the deck, where he lay down and fell into a deep sleep. (Jonah 1:5)

Two key things happen as life unravels: The first is when we run from God, we stop hearing His voice.

WHEN WE RUN FROM GOD, WE STOP HEARING HIS VOICE.

While the sailors tried everything to save themselves and the ship, Jonah hid below deck. This crew prayed to multiple gods, hoping one of them could stop the storm and winds. They even sacrificed the precious cargo, tossing it overboard to lighten the load. Meanwhile, Jonah was down in his cabin, a quilt pulled over his head, hoping he could dream the whole thing away. He stopped hearing from God.

Even though Jonah stopped listening to God's words, God would get his attention anyway. The wind, the rain, the storms, the hurdles, and the roadblocks seemed to be working against Jonah and his fellow passengers on that ship.

Have you ever felt like the whole world was against you? I certainly have. Frustrations, conflicts, problems, and challenges all sometimes drive me crazy when trying to accomplish something else. I'm amazed how God will always keep working to get our attention, one way or another. As if the storm alone wouldn't wake Jonah, a person on the ship confronted him.

The captain went to him and said, "How can you sleep? Get up and call on your god! Maybe he will take notice of us so that we will not perish." (Jonah 1:6)

YOU CAN
TRY TO
RUN FROM
GOD, BUT
YOU
CANNOT
OUTRUN
GOD.

The captain, who I assume did not yet believe in God, had to drag Jonah out of bed and yell at him to get back on deck to help. He instructed Jonah to do the last thing he wanted: Pray to his God!

Then the sailors said to each other, "Come, let us cast lots to find out who is responsible for this calamity." They cast lots, and the lot fell on Jonah. (Jonah 1:7)

Think of this as a random draw. In ancient times, people often used these types of "lots" to discern what to do next. I am not sure exactly how a game of dice was played on the deck of a ship in a terrible storm. Nonetheless, the lot fell on Jonah, meaning that God used their system to reveal Jonah and his disobedience as the cause of the storm. Jonah was the real reason for all this happening. He placed all their lives at risk.

So they asked him, "Tell us, who is responsible for making all this trouble for us? What kind of work do you do? Where do you come from? What is your country? From what people are you?" (Jonah 1:8)

It was revealed that Jonah was somehow the cause of the storm. They asked those questions in desperation, as if they were asking, "What in the world could you have done to make your god so angry at you?"

He answered, "I am a Hebrew and I worship the Lord, the God of heaven, who made the sea and the dry land." (Jonah 1:9)

God called Jonah on a special mission, but he ran away in the opposite direction. Not only was he a coward, but he also brought the sailors within a heartbeat of a watery grave. God entrusted Jonah with a special assignment, and yet Jonah disregarded God. These men eventually became believers in Jonah's God, but it was not because Jonah was a good witness!

There was not much about Jonah that inspired anyone on the ship. He fled and hid from one problem, only to cause an even bigger one. In the end, all these sailors became believers in the one true God! The final scene explains how this happened, but it was unexpected.

This terrified them, and they asked, "What have you done?" (They knew he was running away from the Lord because he had already told them so.) (Jonah 1:10)

A second thing that often happens when life is unraveling: When we run from God, we often hurt the people closest to us.

When someone runs away from God, those around them can suffer negative consequences. Our families, friends, and even those we are called to love and serve

WHEN WE RUN FROM GOD, WE OFTEN HURT THE PEOPLE CLOSEST TO US.

can suffer if we disobey God and run away from our calling.Jonah didn't even realize that all these men are placed in great danger because of his disobedience. How about you and me? Have we ever run away from God and didn't even realize that those around us might suffer because of that?

These sailors threw cargo overboard, broke ropes, and watched their sails being torn apart. They were taking losses and could have drowned. If they arrived at the port of Tarshish, they would have lost the cargo they were supposed to deliver. They might have lost their jobs. Why? Because they allowed a guy named Jonah, who was running from God, to purchase a ticket onto their boat. That is all. God had a special assignment for Jonah, but he put all these people in danger by running away.

Friends, let me tell you something: Your decisions will affect your family, friends, coworkers, teammates, and others closest to you. When we run from God and life unravels, we stop hearing from Him, and we often see those closest to us get hurt. At this point, this ordeal had not just put Jonah in danger; it had put everyone around him in danger as well.

The sea was getting rougher and rougher. So they asked him, "What should we do to you to make the sea calm down for us?" (Jonah 1:11)

Once the sailors realized Jonah was the person to blame, they interrogated him about how to fix this terrible situation. They had tried everything, and the wind and waves splashed higher and harder. Jonah knew what to do: His worst nightmare was precisely what he and everyone else needed.

JONAH'S WORST NIGHTMARE WAS PRECISELY WHAT HE AND EVERYONE ELSE NEEDED.

"Pick me up and throw me into the sea," he replied, "and it will become calm. I know that it is my fault that this great storm has come upon you." (Jonah 1:12)

Finally, Jonah owned his disobedience, confessed, and faced his worst nightmare. Put yourself in Jonah's place for a moment. He finally admitted what he had done and conceded that this was probably the end of his life. But these sailors tried once more to save everyone, including Jonah.

Instead, the men did their best to row back to land. But they could not, for the sea grew even wilder than before. (Jonah 1:13)

Interestingly, these sailors did not throw Jonah into the sea the first chance they got. They made one more effort to dig their oars into the swelling waves with the hope that they could paddle back to shore. They did not want to kill Jonah by throwing him overboard. A bunch of seasoned sailors knew that if they threw him overboard in a storm like this, he would die. Eventually, throwing Jonah overboard was their final and desperate choice.

Then they cried out to the Lord, "Please, Lord, do not let us die for taking this man's life. Do not hold us accountable for killing an innocent man, for you, Lord, have done as you pleased."
(Jonah 1:14)

They did not want to sacrifice Jonah, but there didn't seem to be any other alternative. So, as they dangled him over the deep water, they cried out to God for forgiveness. If this Jonah guy was innocent, they did not want to be punished for drowning him! It's interesting also that they seem to be addressing the real God here. Notice the capital L in the word Lord!

I have often wondered why Jonah didn't volunteer to just jump overboard when the storm didn't stop. He was obviously in a very low place as he had disobeyed God, and everyone knew it. Of all the people on the boat, Jonah knew God and had a relationship with Him. He had spoken and taught on God's behalf in the past! Now that the truth was exposed, he might have felt paralyzed. He knew

he had made a serious mistake in disobeying God, so he accepted his punishment and was ready to die in the sea.

Then they took Jonah and threw him overboard, and the raging sea grew calm. (Jonah 1:15)

Jonah was right, the storm stopped when he owned his sin and accepted the consequences.

At this the men greatly feared the Lord, and they offered a sacrifice to the Lord and made vows to him. (Jonah 1:16)

The ship went from a watery coffin to a floating revival service! God calmed the storm. The crew was saved and put their faith in God; this crew went from lost pagans to full-blown believers in the God of Israel.

This was not because Jonah was brave, impressive, or charismatic, but because he accepted responsibility and quit running away. He faced the truth and offered to save the ones he had put in danger. The story of Jonah is often compared to the story of Jesus. Jesus also willingly died on the cross to stop our storms. Jesus owned our sin and saved us when we were the lost sailors. In this way, the prophet Jonah and his story point us directly to Jesus! Jesus came into the world to lead us back to God. Ever since Adam and Eve, all of humanity has been running away. This story foreshadows God's love for all people and how He uses men and women to work out His plans.

As we read on, we discover that Jonah did not drown! This was not the end of this fascinating story. God was with Jonah even when all hope seemed lost. I can imagine Jonah was sinking, believing

GOD LOVES
YOU SO
MUCH THAT
HE DOES
NOT CHASE
YOU—
HE GOES
AHEAD OF
YOU!

that he would drown. One of my greatest fears is sinking into dark, bottomless water or having to swim to safety in a stormy sea. This was a horrible and terrifying place for Jonah to be.

God sent a fish large enough to swallow Jonah whole so that he didn't drown and it was an unbelievable act of grace and mercy. He was rescued from death!

Now the Lord provided a giant fish to swallow Jonah, and Jonah was in the belly of the fish three days and three nights.
(Jonah 1:17)

This is a tough part of the story to understand and explain. A giant fish swallowed Jonah, and he would spend the next three days and nights inside that fish. This seemed like the bad news, but there was good news also.

God stays involved in our lives not to pay us back, but to bring us back.

God does not sit in heaven with folded arms, waiting and watching for us to mess up so that He can punish us. If you think this, your image of God is all wrong. He is not a harsh, stern, heavenly Father waiting

> **GOD STAYS INVOLVED IN OUR LIVES NOT TO PAY US BACK, BUT TO BRING US BACK.**

to correct us. You probably have made mistakes or tried to run away from God , but please remember this: God loves you so much that He does not chase you—He goes ahead of you!

God went ahead of Jonah and planned to save him from the sea. He also goes ahead of you and me because He has an exciting plan for us. God will reach down to us, even in the darkest moments when we feel we are sinking. He will be there when we feel fear, shame, guilt, anger, or loneliness.

In the following few pages, we see Jonah running back toward God! In the stomach of that giant fish, Jonah found forgiveness and was finally ready to obey God's instructions.

CHAPTER 1 QUIZ

1. You can try to _____ away from God, but you cannot _____ God.

2. God may ask _____ to do things you do _____ want to do.

3. You can always find a _____ sailing in the _____ direction if you really want one.

4. We often run to _____ and _____ places.

5. When we run away from God, _____ begins to _____.

6. When we run from God, we stop _____ His voice.

7. When we run from God, we often _____ the people closest to us.

8. Jonah's worst _____ was precisely what he and everyone else needed.

9. God stays involved in our lives not to _____ us back, but to _____ us back.

10. God loves you so much that He does not _____ you — He goes _____ of you!

QUESTIONS FOR REFLECTION & DISCUSSION

1. Have you ever felt like God was prompting you to do something you did not want to do? Have you been called to a Nineveh?

_____

_____

_____

_____

2. If so, how did you obey God? Have you ever tried to run away from God?

_____

_____

_____

_____

3. If you have ever run away from God, were there hurdles or "storms" that He put in your path to bring you back?

_____

_____

_____

_____

A PRAYER WHEN WE RUN AWAY FROM GOD

Dear Lord,

I know I've tried to run from Your plans. Like Jonah, I've turned away, seeking my own path, but I realize I can't escape Your presence.

I confess my disobedience in _____.

Forgive me and help me trust in Your wisdom.

I'm sorry for using _____ as a distraction.

Give me the courage to turn back to You and follow Your lead.

If _____ is my "Nineveh," clarify that for me.

Thank you for Your mercy and for never giving up on me.

Guide me back to You with an obedient heart.

Amen.

You can try to run away from God, but you cannot outrun God.

_____

_____

_____

_____

_____

_____

_____

_____

_____

_____

_____

_____

_____

_____

_____

CHAPTER 2

RUNNING BACK TO GOD

Now the Lord provided a giant fish to swallow Jonah, and Jonah was in the belly of the fish three days and three nights.
(Jonah 1:17)

In my mind, chapter two of Jonah should start with the verse above. I don't know who separated this in the biblical formatting, but we will start here.

Think back to the first chapter, Jonah ran in the opposite direction of where God told him to go, and there was a terrible storm. When the sailors on the boat panicked, Jonah said, "I'm the problem." Jonah came to his senses, confessed his sins, and the men on the boat were saved. He was thrown overboard and probably assumed he would drown, but God had other plans. He sent a fish to swallow Jonah, which saved him from certain death.

God doesn't let this crisis go to waste. He had Jonah's complete attention for three days while he was stuck in the belly of a giant fish. Can you imagine? God had saved Jonah from drowning, but Jonah had a choice here, as we will see. When we run away from God and things have completely fallen apart, we always have a choice.

GOD WAS NOT PAYING BACK JONAH FOR HIS SIN, BUT BRINGING JONAH BACK FROM HIS SIN.

During this part of the story, I want you to consider that God was not paying back Jonah FOR his sin, but bringing Jonah back FROM his sin.

From inside the fish, Jonah prayed to the Lord his God. (Jonah 2:1)

Duh! Of course he did. Even when life looks the worst it could ever be, it is never too late to pray.

About 45 seconds earlier, Jonah was trying to run away from God, but now he came back to God in prayer, inside the digestive system of a big fish. This moment of stress in the most unlikely place, is a powerful reminder of the transformative effect of prayer. It's not about the location, the circumstances, or even our words, but simply the heart that turns to God in prayer.

Do you think it is interesting that Jonah came back to God now? He wasn't interested in talking to God while on the ship in the storm, while he was on dry land back at Joppa, or when he first heard God's instructions. Those would have been GREAT times and places to pray. Fortunately for Jonah, it is never too late to pray!

We are no different. We pray when we find ourselves in challenging situations, but also in the smaller difficulties we face. Recently, I was at the dentist's office and needed to have very serious repair work done on one tooth. I was nowhere near death, but I prayed. "Lord, please hear me and give me relief and make this end soon."

GOD'S LOVE

IS

UNWAVERING AND

UNCONDITIONAL.

Some of you might be in trouble right now. Maybe you're in a conflict with your parents, or struggling with addiction, depression, or anxiety. Perhaps you have been through terrible trauma. Sometimes, it does not matter what we believe about God, but we find ourselves crying out to Him, just like Jonah.

What did he pray? What does a person in this kind of mess say to God? We can learn a lot from Jonah through his prayer.

He said: "In my distress I called to the Lord, and he answered me. From deep in the realm of the dead, I called for help, and you listened to my cry." (Jonah 2:2)

Jonah describes his situation as "from deep in the realm of the dead." That a pretty dark place, but it is never too late to pray. God hears our cries because He loves us. Swallowed by a fish, stuck in total darkness and utterly alone, Jonah did the one thing we all need to do when we hit rock bottom: he cried out to God.

Do you believe that? We often think that if we are good, God will hear us, but then, when we are bad, God ignores or holds back from us. We make our faith in God more like a transaction than a relationship, but this is not true!

God's love is unwavering and unconditional.

When my three daughters were young, I was honored to be our home's bedtime story, song, and prayer guy. I was blessed to connect with each of them one-on-one for just a couple of minutes each evening at bedtime, and I remember one night I purposely asked Shannon, our oldest (she was 10 or 11 years old), a question. I knew she had gotten into trouble earlier that day. It was just a bad day. I asked her if she thought that I loved her more when she was good or when she had been bad. She quickly answered that she thought I would love her more when she was *good*.

I said to her, "I love you the same *either way*. You cannot do anything that would ever make me love you more or do anything to make me love you any less." I told her this was exactly how God loves us also, no matter what we do.

God will always hear us because He always loves us.

We can hold onto this truth no matter what we've done or where we find ourselves. God's love is not based on our actions, but rather on His character. He loves us unconditionally and is always ready to hear our prayers.

> **GOD WILL ALWAYS HEAR US BECAUSE HE ALWAYS LOVES US.**

When we believe in Jesus and accept His love and forgiveness in our lives, we become children of God. We are not hired employees or like someone who rents a room from a landlord. Those are transactional relationships. We do our part, and we expect God to do His part. Those are superficial and surface relationships at best. Being a child of God is unique; it's different and more profound. That is what makes Jonah's story even more powerful. He is a child of God running back to his Father, even though it's probably pretty cramped inside the belly of that fish.

The miracle of prayer is that we can talk to God and He listens to us, ready to understand, guide, and comfort us. Much like a father loves his children no matter what, God loves us even more.

I do not care if you have been in church your whole life or if this is the first Christian type book you have ever read. If you feel like you are running away from God, you need to know that God is listening and hears you, even in the depths of the pain, the shame, and the despair. Prayer is the way we can run back to God every time.

Jonah continued his prayer:

"You hurled me into the depths, into the very heart of the seas, and the currents swirled about me; all your waves and breakers swept over me." (Jonah 2:3)

Wait, I thought it was the men on the boat who threw Jonah overboard, but I guess it was God afterall. Jonah remembers that God created waves in the sea, created the air, even created the fish.

God will get our attention! I have often "run away" and gotten myself into some messes. When I look back, I can see God's hand guiding me. His presence and plan go before us, even when we don't realize it.

John Ortberg, a Christian author, speaker, and pastor, said, "God is into redeeming things. He is the finder of directionally challenged sheep, the searcher of missing coins, and the embracer of foolish prodigal children. God's favorite department is the "lost and found" department."

Jonah was in the darkest and most dangerous place he had ever been, literally inside the stomach of fish in the middle of the sea! I cannot imagine a worse situation for a human, can you? That was as lost as you can get. No matter how lost you feel, Jonah's story teaches us that God's grace and forgiveness are guaranteed.

Jonah probably felt like he was sinking down to his death, but through this prayer, he began to look "up".

"I said, 'I have been banished from your sight, yet I will look again toward your holy temple.' The engulfing waters threatened me; the deep surrounded me; seaweed was wrapped around my head. To the *roots of the mountains* I sank; the earth beneath barred me in forever. But you, Lord my God, brought my life up from the pit." (Jonah 2:4–6, emphasis added)

His memory of the whole ordeal probably came back to his mind. He went down to Joppa to hop on that ship. He went down into the hull of the ship to sleep.

He went down to the "roots of the mountains", which is pretty far down! The deepest part of the Mediterranean Sea is over 17,000 feet deep. Did that fish swim to the bottom of the sea? Does anyone else have an irrational fear of deep water, like me?

Like Jonah, any time we run away from God, our lives will only go *down*—even 17,000 feet. We cannot even imagine how deep that is! (It is about 3.5 miles, actually.)

"I said, 'I have been banished from your sight, yet I will look again toward your holy temple.'" (Jonah 2:4)

Why did he pray that part about the temple? The answer is a very interesting part of the backstory.

King Solomon built the religious temple that Jonah is speaking about. It was God's holy temple in Jerusalem! When King Solomon built that temple, he spoke some fascinating and powerful words at the dedication ceremony:

"and when a prayer or plea is made by anyone among your people Israel—being aware of the afflictions of their hearts, and

spreading out their hands toward this temple—then hear from heaven, your dwelling place. Forgive and act; deal with everyone according to all they do, since you know their hearts (for you alone know every human heart)." (1 Kings 8:38–39)

Jonah was running back to God and was genuinely repenting! He had become very aware of his heart's affliction and was spreading his hands (even from inside a giant fish) toward the temple of God where he had visited and worshipped! Remember that Jonah had three days and nights to think and pray. I would say that's enough time to search your soul deeply.

"When my life was ebbing away, I remembered you, Lord, and my prayer rose to you, to your holy temple." (Jonah 2:7)

Jonah prayed to God alone, not toward Tarshish or his home but toward God's holy temple—where he knew God was.

"Those who cling to worthless idols turn away from God's love for them." (Jonah 2:8)

Now, that is quite a statement. I can't imagine what it would be like to be stuck inside a giant fish. Cramped and unbelievably horrible, I'm sure. Jonah prayed an interesting sentence here, reminding us that our perspective changes in terrible situations. The things that were so important to us aren't nearly as valuable anymore. Jonah's story demonstrates that clinging to something worthless turns us away from God's love and care.

What was the worthless idol that Jonah might have been thinking of? It could have been his comfortable home or the easy life doing whatever he wanted. What worthless idols in your life tempt you to turn away from God's love? For some of us, it's money, influence, or popularity. We want these things more than we want to please God.

From inside that terrible, dark, and lost place, Jonah decided again what was most important in life.

"But with shouts of grateful praise, I will sacrifice to you. What I have vowed I will make good. I will say, 'Salvation comes from the Lord.'" (Jonah 2:9)

As a child, I could be very annoying, escpecially to my younger sister. Can you relate? I was high-energy, fairly quick-witted and loved to explore and compete. I could get myself into serious trouble. With my dad out working, my mom sometimes would spank me. I can honestly say now that I deserved the punishment. At the time, I would do anything to get out of it. As soon as my mom would reach for the plastic spatula or wooden spoon, I was a changed kid! I would say, "Wait, Mom, I'm a new boy!"

My mom would say, "Yes, son, I hear you. I understand you're sorry, but you're still getting a spanking." Good parents want us to remember the strong connection between our rebellion and something unpleasant. My mom loved me so much that she made sure I understood the consequences for whatever mischief I had committed, probably against my younger sister. I am thankful for that today, by the way.

GOD'S DISCIPLINE IS THOROUGH, BUT IT IS ALSO THOUGHTFUL.

Although God's grace and love for us are guaranteed, He knows us too well. He even knows how you and I will learn lessons. He wants us to know that there are consequences for our actions, but He loves us and cares enough to bring us back. There is another truth here you need to understand. God's discipline is thorough, but it is also thoughtful.

God left Jonah in the belly of that fish for *three* days. Even just one minute would have probably done the trick for you and me. God dismissed Adam and Eve from the Garden of Eden for disobeying just that little command about the trees and fruit. In the Old Testament, God warned the nation of Israel over and over to obey Him. Often, He allowed them to be punished, taken captive, and even exiled. God's love never fails us; His discipline always has a purpose.

Here is how the author of Hebrews explained it:

Moreover, we have all had human fathers who disciplined us, and we respected them for it. How much more should we submit to the Father of spirits and live? They disciplined us for a little while as they thought best, but God disciplines us for our good so that we may share in his holiness. No discipline seems pleasant at the time, but painful. Later on, however, it produces a harvest of righteousness and peace for those trained by it. (Hebrews 12:9–11)

If something difficult is going on in your life right now, you might feel like you are being disciplined. Jonah knew how that felt, and he never forgot this experience. When you are in over your head, you need to realize where you are, admit what is true, and turn back toward God.

Whatever discipline you might be receiving right now, I promise you it is not meant to punish you for no reason. Jonah's story reminds us that God is not *paying* you back—He is *bringing* you back. Although discipline will be painful, it is the way we grow. Comfort and growth don't often live together in our lives. Each time I have prayed for God to give me wisdom, He did not just "give me wisdom". He answered those prayers with experiences and "real life" that allowed me to learn and grow in wisdom over time.

Jonah came to the end of his prayer:

"But I, with shouts of grateful praise, will sacrifice to you. What I have vowed I will make good. I will say, 'Salvation comes from the Lord.'" (Jonah 2:9)

Jonah decided to make good on his vow, his promise to follow the Lord and do what God instructed. He understood on a whole new level that "salvation comes from God". No one could help him in the depths of the sea – not his friends, parents, or anyone on dry land. God was his only hope, but He was also all Jonah needed! Salvation indeed comes from the Lord. That is not just the theme of Jonah's story; the entire Bible tells that good news!

Here is the last truth in chapter two: God gives second chances.

GOD GIVES SECOND CHANCES.

The Lord commanded the fish, and it vomited Jonah onto dry land. (Jonah 2:10)

God commanded that the fish spit Jonah back up onto the shoreline. I do not fully understand how that happened, but I believe it did. Jonah had survived and was without a doubt overjoyed to return to dry land.

Let us take a little peek at just one verse in chapter three. It is an awesome, life changing verse. One that all of us should memorize:

Then the word of the Lord came to Jonah a second time:
(Jonah 3:1)

To me, this is one of the most significant verses in the entire Bible! God gives second, third, and one-hundredth chances. After all the trouble, all the running and shame, all the praying and repenting, Jonah got another chance. God's word came to him *AGAIN!*

God is the God of multiple chances! We must not take advantage of that. You can trust that no matter how deep you may have sunk, God still has a plan and a purpose for your life. This is because He loves you.

God's love for us is deep and wide. Even when we turn away and try to run from Him, His love for us doesn't change.

Run back to God today. Do not wait. Turn back to Him in the midst of your mess and make good on your promise to follow Him!

A REVIEW QUIZ

1. God gives _____ chances.

2. God was not paying back Jonah _____ his sin, but bringing Jonah back _____ his sin.

3. God's love is unwavering and _____.

4. God always _____ us because He always _____ us.

5. Clinging to something _____ turns us away from God's _____ and care.

6. God's discipline is _____, but it is also _____.

QUESTIONS FOR REFLECTION & DISCUSSION

1. How do you think God uses our "belly of the fish" moments to bring us back to Him? Can you recall when you felt God was giving you a second chance?

_____

_____

_____

_____

2. How does this part of the story change your perspective on prayer and seeking God, even during our deepest troubles?

_____

_____

_____

_____

3. What steps can you take to acknowledge your mistakes, seek God's mercy, and ensure you are moving forward, obeying His will?

_____

_____

_____

_____

A PRAYER FOR RUNNING BACK TO GOD

Dear Lord,

Even in my lowest moments, I know You have not abandoned me.

I confess my sins and am grateful for Your love and forgiveness, reaching into my failures and fears.

I acknowledge my disobedience in the areas of _____ _____.

Thank you for the discipline that restores me, not to punish but to help me.

I appreciate the second chances You provide and the assurance that You love me.

Grant me the courage to follow wherever You lead,

trusting in Your unfailing love and grace.

Amen.

God gives second chances.

_____

_____

_____

_____

_____

_____

_____

_____

_____

_____

_____

_____

_____

_____

_____

_____

_____

_____

CHAPTER 3

RUNNING WITH GOD

I am not particularly good at golf. Continuing to play has taught me a lot of patience!

In golf, there is a term called a mulligan. It is when you hit a bad shot, like into the water or off into the woods, and your partner or opponent says, "Nah, that doesn't count. Why don't you take another shot?" It's a second chance, a "do-over" that is so helpful when we've made a mistake.

This story of Jonah, a man who received a huge mulligan in life, resonates with all of us. We've all made mistakes and have needed a second chance. In that sense, our lives may resemble Jonah's, and we can find comfort in knowing that we are not alone when we fail in our faith journey.

Then the word of the Lord came to Jonah a second time:
(Jonah 3:1)

After all that Jonah had done, running away, causing harm to himself, and even risking the lives of those around him, he descended into a deep, dark place. With nowhere else to turn, his heart returned to God through a beautiful prayer, and the fish spat him back onto the sandy seashore. God gave him another chance as the sunshine and fresh sea air revived him.

He got a mulligan!

I cannot overemphasize this. This story is not about how far away we can get from God, but a story about God's love and forgiveness in Jonah's life. It is also a story about the love and grace that God extended to an evil group of people, the citizens of Nineveh. Oh yeah, remember them?

You might believe the bad things that you have done are unforgivable. You might say, "Yeah, but you don't know what I've done."

As a pastor, I often meet people who say they understand that God forgives them through Jesus' shed blood and death, but they can't seem to forgive themselves. I frequently reply, "Really? Let's think through that for a minute. Who told you that you were in charge of forgiving you? Who gave you the right to judge yourself?" The only logical answer to these questions is – the devil.

If you feel that God could never forgive you or use you after some things you have done, I am here to tell you that that is a lie. It is a lie that the devil wants you to believe. Whenever the devil reminds you of your past, remind him of his future! (It is not pleasant!) His future is to be destroyed by Jesus. This book is written to tell you this truth, which I believe with all my heart: God's second chances are not limited by our past actions or perceived unworthiness.

God can use you no matter how bad you think you have been. Even after a moral failure, God can use you. If you've struggled with addiction, He is the God of second chances. Read this carefully:

God gave a second chance to this prophet named Jonah, who lived all those years ago in the Bible and disobeyed Him. This power of God's forgiveness should inspire hope in us, knowing that God's love and grace are always available to us.

Another interesting point that we need to realize is this: God didn't change the assignment.

God gave Jonah a second chance, but the instructions remained the same. He said, "Go to Nineveh." He knew that Jonah did not want to go there. He knew Jonah

GOD DIDN'T CHANGE THE ASSIGNMENT.

had run away in the opposite direction the first time. God spoke again to Jonah, but the message did not change:

"Go to the great city of Nineveh and proclaim to it the message I give you." (Jonah 3:2)

The instructions from God were the same in chapter three as they were in chapter one. God did not back down or change His mind. He never said to Jonah, "Aww, you poor guy, I guess I'll send someone else," or "I know you've been through so much; I will change my plan for you." No. Jonah's mission to go to Ninevah was the same!

When my daughters were little, sometimes they were disobedient, much like all kids. For example, even though they went to bed at the same time every night, they would fall apart when we said it was time for bed. They would flop around on the floor, throw a fit, or want another story, one more drink of water, or ask just one more question. When this happened, my wife and I would tell them two simple things. First, "You can throw a fit all you want; you can try to distract us or fight it. That is fine. However, secondly, you are STILL going to bed." We didn't waiver, or change our minds.

GOD'S **SECOND**

CHANCES **ARE**

NOT **LIMITED**

BY OUR PAST

ACTIONS OR

PERCEIVED

UNWORTHINESS.

God also treated Jonah that way. He might have said, "Jonah, you can try to run away, you can throw a fit and try to fight me on this, but it is TIME to go to Nineveh!"

Delayed obedience does not change the instructions.

DELAYED OBEDIENCE DOES NOT CHANGE THE INSTRUCTIONS.

As we continue reading, Jonah finally made his way to the city of Ninevah. Consider this, if God had gone to all this trouble, the citizens of Nineveh must have really needed this message, and Jonah must have been an **outstanding** preacher, right?

We know from Old Testament Bible scholars that to travel from the seashore to Nineveh would have taken several weeks to walk. Jonah had a lot of time to walk and think, talking to God about the right message, thinking about how best to say the words to the people of Ninevah. He must have thought of all the brilliant illustrations he would use and the right locations and people he would talk to. He must have planned so well that his message to them was going to be amazing! As a pastor, this is what I would have been thinking.

Jonah began by going a day's journey into the city, proclaiming, "Forty more days and Nineveh will be overthrown." (Jonah 3:4)

That's it. Wait, what? There was no opening, fancy presentation, or well thought out, passionate preaching. Just. Eight. Simple. Words. And?

The Ninevites believed God. A fast was proclaimed, and all of them, from the greatest to the least, put on sackcloth. When Jonah's warning reached the king of Nineveh, he rose from his throne, took off his royal robes, covered himself with sackcloth and sat down in the dust. (Jonah 3:5–6)

In Bible times, wearing sackcloth, ash, and dust were signs of great sorrow and repentance. Let's review. Jonah, a Jewish stranger to the people of Ninevah, walked into this large city full of evil people, spoke a simple eight-word phrase, and everyone, including the king, heard and believed him. They repented!

It would be like you or me walking into downtown Cleveland, Ohio, shouting, "Forty more days and Cleveland will be overthrown!" Then we drop the microphone. That is what Jonah did.

The King of Nineveh even made a decree:

This is the proclamation he issued in Nineveh: "By the decree of the king and his nobles: Do not let people or animals, herds or flocks, taste anything; do not let them eat or drink. But let people and animals be covered with sackcloth. Let everyone call urgently on God. Let them give up their evil ways and their violence. Who knows? God may yet relent and with compassion turn from his fierce anger so that we will not perish." (Jonah 3:7–9)

Strangely, the king's declaration sounds very similar to Jonah's prayer from inside the fish. How did this simple message work so well? Who could use one simple statement and convince everyone to repent and turn from their wicked ways? That would be God.

If we do a little historical research into the city and the times, guess who we find? God.

Some scholars believe some terrible things were happening to the city in and around the same time Jonah arrived: Two plagues had killed many people in the city and the surrounding kingdoms. History recorded these to have happened in 765 BC and 759 BC. A solar eclipse had also occurred, which frightened many who did not understand it. Astronomers estimate this would have happened in 763 BC. Enemy warrior tribes continuously attacked the city for many years, and historical archives mention that the city was in economic decline.

Finally, even Jonah showing up might have caused alarm. Some scientists and Bible scholars believe that if a man were in the stomach of a fish for three days, his skin and hair may have been affected. He might have looked like a ragged, bleached zombie walking into the city!

For context, a king ruled a grand city with hundreds of thousands of people. They were managing two fatal plagues and losing many of their people to sickness. There were changes in the sun and the sky, and the threat of their enemies coming to overtake them. Do you see what was happening there? This is what we have been talking about the whole time! Throughout this story, God was at work in the hearts of the people of Nineveh way before Jonah ever arrived.

God had prepared them to hear Jonah's message: "Forty more days, and you're all going to be overthrown." It probably didn't matter what Jonah said as long as it was a directive like "repent and believe."

They repented and believed in God. They were sorry and wanted to change. Done deal.

Not because Jonah had selected just the right way to bring the message. Not because he was an excellent speaker who crafted just the most effective, logical, or philosophical argument to convince everyone. God had prepared the circumstances and their hearts to hear the message ahead of time. We need to remember that God is working in the lives of everyone we meet.

If and when God prompts us to speak to someone about Jesus or invite them to a church event, we should not back down. Remember your Nineveh? Remember the calling and purpose that God may have given you? God is preparing the way for you to execute His plans.

GOD IS WORKING IN THE LIVES OF EVERYONE WE MEET.

Someone you know may look like they have it together on the outside, but looks can be deceiving. They might seem like they would be offended if you bring up God in your conversation with them, but God is always at work.

Jonah entered a powerful, menacing city, but God was already working in the hearts of the people there. Nineveh did not look like a city ready to turn from the wickedness it was known for. The Assyrians living there were some of the meanest, harshest people from this time period in history. The Assyrian people looked like they would never have been open to Jonah's message, but they were, because God had gone ahead of Jonah.

God is always at work, doing things you and I may not see so that people will be open and ready to hear His message. I know this from experience. If God has genuinely asked you to do something, why would you think He hasn't prepared you and a way to accomplish it? Even though Jonah didn't think he was the right person for the job, God knew that he was the right choice.

Look at it this way, we do not start at step one with anyone. We join God where He is already working!

WE DO NOT START AT STEP ONE WITH ANYONE. WE JOIN GOD WHERE HE IS ALREADY WORKING!

We can get stressed because we need our words to be exactly correct when talking to someone about Jesus, but that isn't the case. We must tell others what we know to be true. Take the time to share graciously and authentically what God has placed on your heart. Share your experience with Him. That's it—no more, no less.

Do you have a coworker, neighbor, classmate, or teammate who needs to connect with God? Perhaps they once believed, but they have walked away from Him.

Don't forget that others are in a process with God. What if you are supposed to be a part of God's plan to bring them into heaven? To change their eternity forever! I promise, God is building a case for belief in their lives. He is already working; we do not start at zero with anyone.

You might think, "Hey, you do not know my neighbor, boss, or family member. They are so very far away from God." Some hardheaded people we know might act like Ninevites! That may be true, but don't ever give up. All God needs from us is the same thing He needed from Jonah: to obey, go, and tell His story, and to follow through with the assignment that He has given to us.

Saint Augustine, a brilliant and deep Christian thinker said, "Without God, we cannot. Without us, God will not."

"WITHOUT GOD, WE CANNOT. WITHOUT US, GOD WILL NOT."

I know that is oversimplified. If we don't do what God instructed, He will probably use someone else! But I hope you catch the point: God wants you to join Him in accomplishing His ultimate plan for the world.

Who will you boldly share Jesus with this week? Has God put someone on your heart? Is there just one person who comes to mind?

You never know where God is at work in other people's lives. Your message may not even be all that sophisticated and polished, but take that first step and share what God has taught you. You might be surprised at the response, God will not be.

When God saw what they did and how they turned from their evil ways, he relented and did not bring on them the destruction he had threatened. (Jonah 3:10)

The chapter ends with a great victory for God. Jonah was the final messenger needed for everyone in the city to repent, change, and become believers!

Sometimes, we might share with someone and not see them fully believe yet, but they are moved a little bit further along in that process because of us. Their interaction with us will be a step in God's plan for them. The apostle Paul wrote about this process:

I planted the seed, Apollos watered it, but God has been making it grow. So neither the one who plants nor the one who waters is anything, but only God, who makes things grow. The one who plants and the one who waters have one purpose, and they will each be rewarded according to their own labor. For we are co-workers in God's service; you are God's field, God's building. (1 Corinthians 3:6–9)

Who is the person or group that God may be calling you to speak to? Is there an injustice in this world that you are passionate about? God may be calling you to be His representative to declare a message and advance His purpose. Is there someone you are called to share a message of hope and love with? Does your Nineveh have a name?

Pray earnestly and then obey passionately what He tells you to do. Always remember that God is responsible for the results.

A REVIEW QUIZ

1. God didn't change the _____.

2. God's _____chances are not limited by our past actions or perceived _____.

3. Delayed _____ does not change the instructions.

4. God is working in the lives of _____ we meet.

5. We do not start at step _____ with anyone. We join God where He is already _____!

6. Without _____, we cannot.

7. Without _____, God will not.

QUESTIONS FOR REFLECTION & DISCUSSION:

1. Looking back at your life, can you identify ways God might have "prepared the soil" long before someone shared the good news with them? How does this perspective change how you view sharing your faith with others?

_____

_____

_____

2. Jonah's message to Nineveh was surprisingly simple—just eight words. How does Jonah's experience challenge the idea that we need to have the "perfect words" or be an "expert" to be used by God?

_____

_____

_____

3. Has God revealed a Nineveh in your life? What are your passions and dreams for this world? How might God call you to serve Him in those places or with those people?

_____

_____

_____

A PRAYER FOR RUNNING WITH GOD

Heavenly Father,

Give me the courage to say "yes" when You call, even when the path is difficult.

Thank you for reminding me that You work in the hearts of those around me. I pray for people in my life who don't yet believe in you.

Help me stay faithful to Your message, trusting Your power is not reliant on my ability.

When I feel inadequate, remind me I'm joining Your work, not starting it.

I lift up these people to you now:

_____

_____

_____

Thank you for allowing me to be part of Your plan to reach others with Your love.

Amen.

CHAPTER 4

RUNNING AGAINST GOD

We have been on quite a journey!

This whole story is pretty short at just forty-eight verses. If the pages of your Bible stick together, you could miss the whole thing!

In chapter four, the story ends, but that ending is unresolved. We learn that Jonah, even after the apparent "success" of his mission trip to Nineveh, disagreed with God forgiving these evil people. For Jonah, this was not what the Ninevites deserved. This led to a fascinating conversation between God and Jonah—one I know I have had with Him also.

Everyone in Nineveh, even the king, repented and believed in God. Jonah's message, as simple as it seemed, was perfect, and they repented, which sounds like a wonderful thing! This whole city repented and believed in the one true God. I'm sure that meant that they would live differently, and probably not be so cruel and evil.

However, there was still a problem with Jonah's heart and mind.

> But to Jonah this seemed very wrong, and he became angry.
> (Jonah 4:1)

JONAH WAS OFFENDED BY GOD'S GRACE.

Jonah was offended by God's grace.

It was as if Jonah said, "I knew this was going to happen."

> He prayed to the Lord, "Isn't this what I said, Lord, when I was still at home? That is what I tried to forestall by fleeing to Tarshish. I knew that you are a gracious and compassionate God, slow to anger and abounding in love, a God who relents from sending calamity." (Jonah 4:2)

He explained that this was why he ran away in the first place! The truth of Jonah's heart was coming to the surface. It wasn't that he was afraid of the Ninevites. He apparently wasn't scared of God either- and he should have been! He was worried that God would forgive them, and he did not want that to happen! Think about that for a moment. Jonah didn't like the Ninevites repenting and being forgiven. To him, it wasn't fair!

At least this is an improvement because he is finally speaking directly to God about the whole situation. I know that sometimes, when I am angry, I forget that I can talk to God.

Isn't this incredible? Jonah had been saved from the raging storm that was caused by his own disobedience, he was rescued from the belly of a fish, he had traveled to preach that little eight-word message, and the whole city was saved. Yet Jonah was somehow angry and indignant toward God. He wanted justice, not forgiveness for the wicked people of Ninevah.

Can you relate? Your story might be similar to Jonah's in that you get angry when things are unfair. We all want God's grace in our lives, but we are offended when God extends grace to someone who we think doesn't deserve it. Let's be honest, Jonah didn't care about the people of Nineveh or what might happen to them. This is why he ran away in the beginning of this story.

God rescued and forgave Jonah! He rescued and forgave us, too. We sing about it in a hymn called "Amazing Grace". It is forgiveness we could never earn. We are the beneficiaries of God's love and grace in our lives. However, when it comes to others, we want to give God a little advice or a commentary on what He should do.

It is as if we say, "Sure, I have done some bad things, and God forgives me. I appreciate the grace in my life. But come on, God, *those* people? Those are the really bad people. You should not forgive *them*." Do we actually think we can receive grace from God, but believe someone else shouldn't receive it as well?

Jonah went even one step further in his mind and heart:

"Now, Lord, take away my life, for it is better for me to die than to live." (Jonah 4:3)

Jonah was saying, "If you won't kill them, then kill me. If that is what you are going to do, God, then just kill me now. Just like back in that huge storm, throw me overboard. I am a dead man, anyway. Just like back in the belly of that huge fish, I am a dead man, Lord. I am so outside of who you are and what you are – just let me go."

Wow, that is such a sad place to be, right?

Our enemy, the devil, deceived Jonah into thinking he was somehow better than the people of Nineveh. Jonah harbored such hatred and unforgiveness for Nineveh that even when they repented and gave honor and worship to God, he couldn't be happy about it— he didn't trust God to make the best decision.

Jesus used an incredible story to teach us about this in Luke 15, the story of the prodigal son. Nineveh was like the younger son, running away and doing sinful things. Jonah was like the older son, resentful when his brother returned home broken and humble. There was a grand celebration for the younger son coming home, but the older son was bitter and wouldn't join the party. In the parable, the father expresses God's love for all people:

"'It was fitting to celebrate and be glad, because this brother of yours was dead and is alive again; he was lost and is found.'"
(Luke 15:32 ESV)

God is with us at our best and worst, but He did not console Jonah. God was a true friend as He spoke to Jonah in this misery:

But the Lord replied, "Is it right for you to be angry?" (Jonah 4:4)

This was a beautiful question. God asked Jonah to think about his own anger. "Do you have a good reason to be this angry?" This question encouraged Jonah to consider *why* he was so angry. We can learn a lot by asking ourselves why we may feel a particular way or have concluded something. I've tried hard to make this a personal discipline when I am upset or angry. We all should try to find what is underneath our emotions. We should ask "Do I have a right to be so angry?"

Isn't it hard when God does this to us? Jesus was so good at doing this while He was on earth. The Gospel stories tell of ways He caused people to think deeply about their lives and decisions.

But Jonah did not answer God here. He walked away from the conversation because he was committed to his comfort.

JONAH WAS COMMITTED TO HIS COMFORT.

Jonah had gone out and sat down at a place east of the city. There he made himself a shelter, sat in its shade and waited to see what would happen to the city. (Jonah 4:5)

Jonah went to a hillside away from the city to sit, think, and watch. This is in an area of the world we now know as Iraq, and it is very hot most of the time. .

Jonah wanted a good view of the city. He assumed that the Ninevites were going to mess up and God would proceed to destroy them after all.

God took this opportunity to try to teach Jonah even more.

Then the Lord God provided a leafy plant and made it grow up over Jonah to give shade for his head to ease his discomfort, and Jonah was very happy about the plant. (Jonah 4:6)

Finally! For the first time in this entire drama, Jonah seemed happy. Sigh. A little shade for his head on a hot day. Jonah felt relieved. Why was that? He was finally comfortable. His needs were being met.

But at dawn the next day, God provided a worm, which chewed the plant so that it withered. When the sun rose, God provided a scorching east wind, and the sun blazed on Jonah's head so that

he grew faint. He wanted to die and said, "It would be better for me to die than to live." (Jonah 4:7-8)

God took away the plant that He had provided. Poor Jonah. He was so angry about the plant and about the city that he just wanted to die! That's pretty angry.

Here is another example of a hard truth we can learn from this part of Jonah's story: Jonah was so consumed with his comfort that God consumed his comfort.

Sometimes, God will remove our comfort so we will hear His calling more clearly.

> **JONAH WAS SO CONSUMED WITH HIS COMFORT THAT GOD CONSUMED HIS COMFORT.**

In the book, The Problem of Pain, author C.S. Lewis said, "God whispers to us in our pleasures, speaks in our consciences, but shouts in our pains. It is his megaphone to rouse a deaf world."

Am I saying God does not want us to be comfortable or have modern conveniences? Of course not! God is okay with your comfort until it begins to hinder your obedience to Him.

God wants to bless all people, but not at the expense of our relationship with Him! If our comfort blinds us to God and His work in and through us, He will intervene. When obedience to Him is at stake, God is willing to make us uncomfortable!

> **GOD IS OKAY WITH YOUR COMFORT UNTIL IT HINDERS YOUR OBEDIENCE TO HIM.**

Jonah lost sight of what God had done around him. He did not see the good work that had been accomplished in Nineveh or recognize how God wanted to use him as a prophet to call people back to Himself.

We, too, can get so caught up in our comfort that we lose sight of God's plan. Sometimes, we get so focused on our grade point average or our success and achievements that we don't notice the person in the cafeteria who just needs a friend to have lunch with. We rush past an opportunity to help an older person in the grocery store or at church because the lines are too long. We get so angry when the internet is down since we can't catch up on social media. Here is what it comes down to: Sometimes what concerns us is different than what concerns God.

I want to challenge you today. An overcommitment to comfort will cause you to miss a lot of God's vision for the world. We live in a world obsessed with our comfort first, then God's plan second, maybe. We must understand that God may have a plan for us to obey Him first

SOMETIMES WHAT CONCERNS US IS DIFFERENT THAN WHAT CONCERNS GOD.

and trust Him no matter what happens, even if we suffer. That is precisely what Jesus modeled for us. Jesus willingly submitted Himself to be punished for our sin. He didn't deserve that—we did. Yet Jesus loved us, all the way to death.

God called Jonah out on this:

But God said to Jonah, "Is it right for you to be angry about the plant?" "It is," he said. "And I'm so angry I wish I were dead." But the Lord said, "You have been concerned about this plant, though you did not tend it or make it grow. It sprang up overnight and died overnight. And should I not have concern for the great city of Nineveh, in which there are more than a hundred and twenty thousand people who cannot tell their right hand from their left— and also many animals?" (Jonah 4:9-11)

It is as if God said, "Jonah, I know that your people and the Ninevites were enemies; and that you have fought with each other. They have hurt you and your people in the past. Should I, God, not be concerned with this great city and all those people who are created in my image? Whose people are they in the first place?"

This whole Jonah story ends with a question. I think it's God's way of telling us that He wants us to be concerned with eternal things.

GOD WANTS US TO BE CONCERNED WITH ETERNAL THINGS.

God said, "Hey, Jonah, you and I are not on the same page. We are not together on this. My concerns and yours are not the same."

God has been saying this to us for a very long time. Another prophet named Isaiah once wrote the following:

"For my thoughts are not your thoughts, neither are your ways my ways," declares the Lord. "As the heavens are higher than the earth, so are my ways higher than your ways and my thoughts than your thoughts." (Isaiah 55:8-9)

Have you ever felt this way? I know I have. I don't understand God's ways all the time. I try to obey God. Sometimes, though, there is a little bit of Jonah in me. Can you relate? There are times when I am trying to get through this life, and I am more concerned with how long the line is at the coffee shop than I am about the people in the line!

I can get so caught up in things that just do not matter—like pizza delivery, a clean car, or the line to get my hair cut—that I have not even considered the eternal souls of the people who are working hard at their jobs to serve me at that moment. How could I share the love of God with them?

God makes a great point with that last question, "Should I not be concerned with all these people who don't know Me?" Yes, Lord, You should be concerned. And so should I. Forgive me for not being on the same page as You.

God wants to remind us that the only thing we can take to heaven is other people.

THE ONLY THING YOU CAN TAKE TO HEAVEN IS OTHER PEOPLE.

In heaven, I am guessing you and I will not wish we had more money, a bigger house, or a fancier car. We will not worry about how many shirts we have in our closet, or cool shoes that we own. These things will not mean anything in heaven. We will not wish that we worked more hours at our jobs, but we will be aware of who is in heaven with us.

I believe Jonah will be in heaven. He was a faithful person who believed in God and served Him, but he wasn't perfect. Because Jonah was obedient, however, the Ninevites will be there also

Who will YOU invite to heaven with you?

God loves that person and may be calling you to visit them with the simple message that God loves them, sees them, and seeks them. In the meantime, listen carefully and obey quickly when God asks you to tell others some excellent news!

WHO

WILL YOU

INVITE

TO

HEAVEN

WITH

YOU?

A REVIEW QUIZ

1. Jonah was _____ by God's grace.

2. Jonah was committed to his _____.

3. Jonah was so _____ with his comfort that God consumed his comfort.

4. God is _____ with your comfort until it hinders your _____ to Him.

5. Sometimes, what concerns _____ is different than what concerns _____.

6. God wants us to be concerned with _____ things.

7. The only thing you can take to heaven is other _____.

8. Who will _____ invite to heaven with you?

QUESTIONS FOR REFLECTION & DISCUSSION

1. Can you think of a time when you struggled to accept God showing grace or favor to someone you felt didn't deserve it? What does this reveal about our understanding of grace?

_____

_____

_____

2. What are some ways that seeking comfort in your own life might be preventing you from following God's calling? How can we balance enjoying God's blessings while remaining open to His direction?

_____

_____

_____

3. How does the thought that you can take people to heaven with you challenge your current priorities and how you spend your time? What might need to change in your life if you truly live with this eternal perspective?

_____

_____

_____

A PRAYER FOR THOSE OPPOSING GOD:

Dear Lord,

Forgive my doubts and resistance to Your plans.

Like Jonah, I struggle to accept Your grace for others while embracing it for myself.

Help me see others as You do, knowing every soul is precious.

When I prioritize comfort over Your calling, remind me that Your thoughts and ways are higher. Grant me an eternal perspective beyond worldly comforts.

Shape my heart to love what You love and celebrate Your love for everyone.

Amen.

Jonah is consumed with his comfort, so God consumed his comfort.

_____

_____

_____

_____

_____

_____

_____

_____

_____

_____

_____

_____

_____

_____

_____

_____

_____

_____

_____

CONCLUSION

Walking and running are great object lessons for life. These are our basic modes of traveling from place to place. Running brings a sense of independence, freedom, and power. The apostle Paul often uses these as an example of our earthly life. We are in a marathon with God. Sometimes, we run away from Him; sometimes, we run back to Him; sometimes, we run against Him. As we reflect on this exploration of the biblical story of Jonah, we are left with a powerful reminder of the importance of God's unwavering love for every person on earth and His desire to partner with us in accomplishing His plans.

God chose Jonah for an incredibly special task – to preach to the people of Nineveh and call them to repentance. Yet, Jonah's human nature got the better of him, and he tried to flee from God's call. Even after he successfully completed the task, Jonah was still angry and depressed, but God was kind and didn't give up on him.

How often do we find ourselves in Jonah's shoes? When God asks us to do something that challenges our comfort zones or goes against our desires, our natural inclination is to resist and run away in the opposite direction. We make excuses, rationalize our disobedience, or ignore the still, small voice of the Divine.

But as Jonah's story vividly illustrates, we cannot escape God's reach. No matter how far we try to run, God's love pursues us, and He will not give up on us. Even in our darkest moments of rebellion and stubbornness, God extends His grace and offers us another chance.

The remarkable thing about the God of the Bible is that His love knows no limits. He loves all people, even those who seem undeserving of His mercy. The people of Nineveh were considered the enemies of God's people, yet when they repented at Jonah's message, God was gracious and spared them from judgment.

This is a powerful testament to the inclusive nature of God's love. He desires that all people, regardless of their background or perceived worth in our eyes, would turn to Him and experience the transformative power of His forgiveness. As the apostle Paul later wrote in the New Testament, "God demonstrates his love for us in this: While we were still sinners, Christ died for us" (Romans 5:8).

The story of Jonah challenges us to listen carefully to God's voice and to strive to obey Him every day. There are risks in this practice. The world may not understand or agree with what we choose to do. This story reminds us that our plans and agendas often pale compared to the grand purposes of the Almighty. When we surrender our will to His, and faithfully follow His leading, we discover that His ways are higher than ours, and His blessings are more significant than anything we could have imagined.

As you reflect on the life of Jonah, may you *dare to believe* in God's call on your life, no matter how daunting or uncomfortable it may seem. Trust in His unfailing love, and know that even when you falter, He will forgive and restore you. May this biblical story inspire you to walk in greater obedience and share the message of God's redemptive love with all whom you encounter.

Pastor Charlie Grimes, December 2024

The
CHARLIE GRIMES
podcast

ENCOURAGEMENT FOR LIFE

Charlie and his wife of 32 years, Wendy, are the proud parents of three daughters and sons-in-law. Charlie is a soundly average golfer who likes to ride his bike, play his guitar, and spend time with his five grandchildren. They reside in Strasburg, Ohio.

WELCOME TO THE SERIES!

Dare to Believe: Discover, Grow, and Live Your Faith.

This first book in the series dives into the core of Christian faith, offering fresh perspectives on classic stories and timeless teachings. Each book provides a unique blend of personal reflection and biblical insights, designed to help you *understand your faith, build your character, connect with your community, and live out your purpose.* Prepare to be challenged, encouraged, and inspired as you journey to become more like Christ.

For teachers and youth pastors: key elements emphasized throughout the Dare to Believe series:

Relatability: Each book uses relatable stories, contemporary language, and real-life examples specifically connecting with youth and young adults.

Practical Application: Each book moves beyond theory and offers clear action steps to help readers grow in their relationship with God, their communities, and themselves.

Authenticity: Each book invites readers into a transparent and honest journey through the complexities of faith.

Encouragement: The series is designed to uplift and empower readers with hope, love, and purpose.

Transformative Learning: The series encourages self-reflection, growth, and a deeper understanding of God's Word.

Please don't leave me on your shelf!
Pass this book along to someone who might
enjoy it!

For additional teaching and encouragement, tune into

The Charlie Grimes Podcast on all popular podcast platforms.

Pastor Charlie maintains an email list with occasional news, special

announcements and encouragement. Sign up on his website:

www.charlesrgrimes.com

YOUR FEEDBACK MATTERS!

Thank you for taking the time to read
this book. Your thoughts and feedback are
incredibly valuable to me. If you enjoyed the
book, please take a moment to leave a review
wherever you are reading! Your review helps
other readers discover the book and supports
my work as an author. Thank you!